Bruce Frederickson

SAINT LOUIS

Series Editors: Thomas J. Doyle and Rodney L. Rathmann

Write to the Library for the Blind, 1333 S. Kirkwood Road, St. Louis, MO 63122-7295 to obtain this study in braille or large print for the visually impaired.

CONTENTS

INTRODUCTION

The Godly Man Series

In his letter to the recently established Christian church at Philippi, the apostle Paul likened the Christian life to a race. Paul wrote, "Forgetting what is behind and straining toward what is ahead, I press on toward the goal to win the prize for which God has called me heavenward in Christ Jesus" (Philippians 3:13–14).

Each of us who by faith claims Jesus as Lord and Savior has God's permission and His power to forget "what is behind." Over 2,000 years ago, Jesus came to earth, true God, Son of the eternal Father and yet True Man. Conceived by the Holy Spirit and born of the Virgin Mary, Jesus grew as a boy—through childhood and adolescence—to become a mature man. He endured all the temptations and struggles every man has faced and yet committed no sin of thought, word, or action. (See Hebrews 4:14–15.) According to His Father's plan, He suffered and died on the cross as our substitute, taking our sins upon Himself. We can forget our sins because Jesus' love has overcome our past. He has won the victory over our sins and the constraining, handicapping power of the devil. Jesus showed Himself Lord over sin, death, and the devil when He rose from the dead on Easter morning. We who believe in the crucified, risen, and ascended Savior are made new men by the same Holy Spirit who brought us to faith. As God's Spirit gives us new desires and a new set of goals and priorities, He changes us through the Word of God—the Gospel—so that we come to know God's love and the outpouring of His grace in mighty ways, and grow in our relationship with our Father in heaven. Long ago, the psalmist wrote by inspiration of the Holy Spirit the following insight into God and His nature, "His pleasure is not in the strength of the horse, nor His delight in the legs of man; the LORD delights in those who fear Him, who put their hope in His unfailing love" (Psalm 147:10–11).

As we run life's race, our heavenly Father invites us to find our strength and encouragement in Him. His joy is not in any physical means by which men may reach a finish line, such as in the power of a horse or the legs of men. Rather, God finds His joy in those sons who put their hope in Him and in the power of His unfailing love.

God's Word reminds us, "[We] are all sons of God through faith in Christ Jesus" (Galatians 3:26) and our God delights in His relationship with His sons just as every good father prides himself in the growth and accomplishments of his children. He invites us to communicate with Him regularly and often as we experience His Word and respond to His love in prayer.

As we press on toward our heavenly prize, God helps us to live our lives for Him. Many of God's faithful people, both men and women, have lived it before us. Theirs is a heritage for us to build upon and to pass on to those who will follow after us— our wives, children, friends, and others whose lives will be touched by the love and power of God evidenced in our lives.

The writer to the Hebrews encourages us to live as men of faith, reminding us about where to keep our focus as we run life's race: "Therefore, since we are surrounded by such a great cloud of witnesses, let us throw off everything that hinders and the sin that so easily entangles, and let us run with perseverance the race marked out for us. Let us fix our eyes on Jesus, the author and perfecter of our faith, who for the joy set before Him endured the cross, scorning its shame, and sat down at the right hand of the throne of God. Consider Him who endured such opposition from sinful men, so that you will not grow weary and lose heart" (Hebrews 12:1–3).

God's blessings as you run the race and claim the prize already won for you!

About the Godly Man Series

The Godly Man series is especially for men. Written in book-study format, each course in the Godly Man series is organized into chapters suitable for either group or individual study. Periodically throughout each chapter, questions have been provided to further stimulate your thinking, assist you in personal application, and spark group discussion.

How to Use Each Course in the Godly Man Series

Each course in the Godly Man series has been prepared especially for small group settings. It may, however, be used as a self-study or in a traditional Sunday morning Bible class. Chapters of each course may be read in advance of group discussion. Or, participants may take turns reading sections of the Bible study during your group study sessions.

Planning for a Small Group Study

1. *Select a leader* for the course or a leader for the day. It will be the leader's responsibility to secure needed materials, to keep the discussion moving, and to help involve all participants.

2. *Emphasize sharing.* Your class will work best if the participants feel comfortable with one another and if all feel their contributions to the class are important and useful. Take the necessary time at the beginning of the course to get to know one another. Since this course deals with relationship issues, you may ask participants to share their names and a little something about a positive relationship they have now or have had in the past. Share what you expect to gain from this course. Develop an atmosphere of openness, trust, and caring among the participants. Agree in advance that private issues shared during your study will remain within the group.

3. *Pray for one another.* Begin and conclude each study session with a prayer. Pray for one another, for your families, your work, and all other aspects of your life. Involve everyone. Consider praying-around-the-circle, with each person offering a specific prayer to God for the person on his left.

As You Plan to Lead the Group

1. Read this guide in its entirety before you lead the first session.

2. Use the Answers and Comments section in the back of the study.

3. Pray each day for those in your group.

4. Depend on the Holy Spirit. Expect His presence; He will guide you and cause you to grow. God will not let His Word return empty (see Isaiah 55:11) as you study it individually or with others in a group.

5. Prepare well, studying each session's material thoroughly. Add your comments in the margins so that you may add your insights to spark conversation and discussion throughout the session.

6. Begin and end the session with prayer.

7. Begin and end on time. Punctuality is a courtesy to everyone and can be a factor to encourage discussion.

8. Find ways to keep the session informal; consider meeting over breakfast at a local restaurant or some other friendly setting where participants can be seated face to face.

9. Keep the class moving. Limit your discussion to questions of interest to the participants. Be selective. You don't need to cover every question. Note that most Bible references are included in the study guide. At times, however, you may want to look up and share additional insights provided by other suggested Bible references.

10. Build one another up through your fellowship and study. Make a conscious effort to support one another in your personal and professional challenges.

Expect and rejoice in God's presence and blessing as He builds your faith and enriches your life through the study of His Word.

PREFACE

Do you remember a time when someone—a parent, teacher, or friend—wanted you to do some work for or with them? Perhaps you were like the second son in the parable Jesus taught. His father asked him to go and work in the family vineyard and he readily agreed. But then he did not go! The first son, however, who at first flatly refused to go and work for his father, later repented and went to work. Why all the emphasis on work?

When two men are introduced they often ask, "What do you do?" When a man is identified in a news story, he is frequently identified by what he does for a living. Remember Tom Sawyer? He certainly expended as much, if not more energy trying to get his friends to do his work, than if he had just done it himself!

Work is important. But is that all there is? When do you have down time? When do you relax? Do you believe it is important to have leisure time? And if so, what do you do for leisure?

Ever since the curse of sin, people have struggled with work. But we don't think much about the curse of leisure. Is there such a thing? If there is, how has it affected you, your family and those with whom you work and play. I believe that God created leisure time so that we can worship Him. I believe He commanded the natural break between work and rest and called it Sabbath because He wanted us to worship Him and enjoy His creation. Don't forget that as one of His more important creatures, He wants you to enjoy yourself.

By God's grace and as a result of studying this course you will be better able to define yourself not merely according to *what* you do, but according to *who* you are. May God give you the insight to carefully examine your own working and playing and to discover new motives for the rest that naturally follows your work. In Jesus ...

Bruce Frederickson

It Is Good! | 1

At the Lake

As I write these words, I am sitting near a large window, overlooking a peaceful lake. I have just spent the winter building this cabin. The work was long, hard, and sometimes cold. It took every one of my days off and some vacation days to do the work, but I enjoyed it. Was this work or was it leisure?

Some mornings when I got up before dawn and worked until after dark, I wondered if I would ever get done. But this morning, I got up and built a fire. I cooked a simple breakfast and brewed a cup of coffee. As I sit here thinking about all the gifts God has given me, I am also struck that among these are included the gifts of relaxation and meditation. God has also given me the gift of leisure—the ability to enjoy the downtime that having a cabin by the lake has brought to my life.

Right now, I resist the temptation to pick up a hammer or a paintbrush and complete the few minor details that remain of this project. And as I turn on my computer to share these words with you, I wonder is this work or play? Is this a job or is it leisure? I know I'm not in my office. This is not my normal work. Writing gives me a task to complete. Yet, it is something I do because I enjoy doing it.

After I have had a brief period of time at the cabin, I return to my usual tasks with a renewed sense of purpose and enthusiasm. I am refreshed, charged up, and ready to get back into my normal routine.

React and Respond

1. What use of your nonplanned time gives you the greatest sense of satisfaction and leaves you feeling refreshed?

2. Mark 1:35 tells how "very early in the morning, while it was still dark, Jesus got up, left the house and went off to a solitary place, where He prayed." Where is your place of solitude when you simply want to be alone to talk with God?

The Gift of Leisure Time

Do you equate unplanned blocks of time with tasks to complete or with things you enjoy doing? For you, does leisure mean just more work, but of a different kind—repair, yard work? People in Bible times and even our immediate ancestors didn't have much time for leisure. They were too busy building their homes, taming the wilderness, and providing food to feed their growing families.

But since the so-called industrial revolution, and certainly in this more recent technological revolution, people seem to have time on their hands, thanks to the labor-saving devices we have been given at the hand of our good and gracious God.

React and Respond

1. For which labor-saving devices are you most thankful?

2. Contrast and compare your lifestyle with that of your parents or grandparents.

Time, the Commodity

We could also argue, however, that people have less leisure time today than a generation ago. Parents—and especially single parents—often juggle home and work commitments in an attempt to provide their children with life's basic necessities while at the same time creating a nurturing home environment. Many people are working an extra job either temporarily or permanently—just to make ends meet. And those ends often justify the desire which seems to grow within us to have more and more. The need for more material things often causes us to devote more time and energy to our work to the end that we have less and less free time in which to enjoy all that we have. Or rather, all that has us.

I remember something my father once said about long distance driving. He said you should stop every two hours and let the car rest! Dad may have seemed more concerned about mechanical things than he was about people. But I think he meant the driver and passengers probably needed a rest every once in a while too.

React and Respond

1. What did your dad or any other adult teach you about the value of rest and relaxation as you were growing up?

2. If you have time on your hands, what do you do with it?

3. Reflect on the question "Are you a human being or a human doing?" What's the difference?

4. Whether we feel we have no time, too much time, or too many options competing for our time, we can say with the psalmist, "My times are in Your hands" (Psalm 31:15). What do the words of psalmist mean to you?

In God We Rest

I am struck with how almost everything in the natural world needs some downtime. We need to rest and shift gears from time to time—to keep fresh to maintain a perspective—and to experience the serenity God created us to enjoy. God did it; why can't we? Or perhaps you can, and I am the odd one!

> By the seventh day God had finished the work He had been doing; so on the seventh day He rested from all His work. And God blessed the seventh day and made it holy, because on it He rested from all the work of creating that He had done. (Genesis 2:2–3)

Do you think that God rested because He was tired, or because He was creating the concept of rest? Clearly God wanted us to take time to cease from our labors to rest our bodies and to focus on Him and His goodness. Deuteronomy 5:12–15 records,

> Observe the Sabbath day by keeping it holy, as the Lord your God has commanded you. Six days you shall labor and do all your work, but the seventh day is a Sabbath to the Lord your God. On it you shall not do any work, neither you, nor your son or daughter, nor your manservant or maidservant, nor your ox, your donkey or any of your animals, nor the alien within your gates, so that your manservant and maidservant may rest, as you do. Remember that you were slaves in Egypt and that the Lord your God brought you out of there with a mighty hand and an outstretched arm. Therefore the Lord your God has commanded you to observe the Sabbath day.

Note that God calls His people Israel to remember the deliverance He provided in freeing them from their bondage in Egypt. Israel's deliverance from slavery foreshadows the deliverance from sin, death, and the devil's power which Jesus earned for us on Calvary's tree. The writer to the Hebrews refers to the gift of salvation that is ours by faith in Jesus as our Sabbath-rest. One day we will enjoy this gift of perfect rest in heaven.

The interesting thing about God proclaiming a Sabbath is that He didn't decree a particular place for each person to observe Sabbath. In Jesus' time, people were so cautious about not breaking God's Third Commandment that they went overboard.

They intensified God's laws with their own ceremonial laws which decreed how far a person could walk or what a person could do on the Sabbath. Actually, many of these extra laws were very helpful because they gave time for people to prepare for Sabbath. But for some, the focus of worshiping God was lost. Jesus put the Sabbath in perspective when He said, "The Sabbath was made for man, not man for the Sabbath" (Mark 2:27).

Jesus also talked about the proper place for worship. A Samaritan woman whom He met at Jacob's well observed: "Our fathers worshiped on this mountain, but you Jews claim that the place where we must worship is in Jerusalem" (John 4:20). Jesus replied, "A time is coming and has now come when the true worshipers will worship the Father in spirit and truth, for they are the kind of worshipers the Father seeks. God is spirit, and His worshipers must worship in spirit and in truth" (John 4:23).

Jesus explained that the Sabbath was a time set aside by God, to allow His people to pause to worship Him. There are a variety of times and places for worship allowed in the Bible. The specific hour or location isn't important, but what happens during the time of worship is crucial. God wants us to focus on Him and to become refreshed with strength, hope, and encouragement He provides us through Word and Sacrament.

Reaction and Response

1. What is worship? Where and when do you most often worship God?

2. Comment on the statement "The man who says he can worship God just as well out on the golf course or in the fishing boat on Sunday morning, usually does."

3. What does the Sabbath mean for the "rhythms and cycles" of your week?

4. In what ways does Sunday worship enrich the rest of your week?

Temple Maintenance

Ivor and Jane and Harry and Sally

Consider Ivor and Jane. They live in what we would call prehistoric times. They have nowhere to go to purchase the items they need to build their shelter. They must work hard to find raw materials. They also need to forage daily for their food since they have no way to keep food fresh—except on the vine! They are constantly on the move since they eat only what grows naturally. Each time they move they build a new shelter close to each new food supply. When the sun comes up, they are out searching, hunting, and protecting themselves from the dangers of wild beasts and the elements. The regular changing of the seasons means appropriate changes in wardrobe, necessary precautions against exposure.

Jane is concerned because she knows she will soon have a child. She wonders how they will ever find enough food to fill even one more mouth! They fall into bed exhausted each night just as the sun sets and dream of just having enough to get by. Ivor and Jane would not understand the concept of leisure time because they've never had any. Their stress is tremendous, especially since a herd of dangerous animals seems to have moved into an area in which they have recently found a good supply of food. Ivor even had a close encounter with one a few days earlier.

Consider their modern counterparts, Harry and Sally. Harry and Sally work hard too. But in different ways. Harry is a computer programmer and Sally is a therapist. Harry occasionally goes into the office early to complete a project that wasn't finished the day before, especially when the boss is asking for it. Sally deals with other people's problems but has only begun to grapple with her own. They recently purchased a new home, and their mortgage payments are large. Sally's patient load is down, as is her income, but she really has no control over it.

Harry stops at the lumberyard on the way home from work to purchase a few items to complete the basement. (They chose to purchase a home with an unfinished basement so they could put some sweat equity into their home.) Jane stops at the grocery store. They meet at the exercise club and share that they are both too tired to cook. So they go out to dinner at a nice restaurant. It is quiet, out of the way, and not too expensive. Over supper they share the events of the day. Harry learns that Sally has found a new dress in the display window next to the grocery store. It will be just perfect for the country club party that weekend, and although she has purchased the dress, she is uncertain how it will affect their finances. Harry confesses that when he stopped at the lumberyard for materials, he purchased a new router which will allow him to be more creative and efficient in completing the basement project.

Harry and Sally express concern because the daily news carried an item about an increase in college tuition which could greatly impact their budget. (They are helping their two children to complete college.) The stress in their life seems tremendous, but they complete the dinner hour conversation with plans for a long-awaited winter vacation in the Caribbean. They also fall into bed exhausted, taking care to set the alarms for their appointments the next day.

React and Respond

1. When have you felt like Ivor and Jane, experiencing stress over just barely having enough to get by?

2. When do you feel like Harry and Sally?

3. It is said that people today actually have *less* leisure time than their parents did a generation ago. When do you most look forward to moments of leisure, which seem all too few and far between?

EXERCISE

Why exercise? At the turn of the century, most people in the United States were living and working on a farm. Today, less than 10 percent live on a farm, and closer to 5 percent actually work on a farm. Large industries which formerly employed thousands of individuals have greatly reduced work forces through industrialization and automation. Robotics can do many functions formerly performed by humans, "working" faster, more accurately, and with no sick leave or vacation time required.

We are living in a rapidly expanding "information age." Most people employed today are handling information rather than objects. Most U.S. workers have jobs related to service rather than production. Today, many workers can comfortably sit in front of a computer terminal and scarcely leave their desk and cubicle. The result? Our bodies are atrophying at an alarming rate. Like machines that rust if unused, we are rapidly becoming the least physically fit society in the history of the world. There seems to be a commensurate increase in health problems which tend to undermine medical advances aimed at increasing life expectancy.

Most people understand the need to keep buildings in good repair. They may not, however, understand and appreciate the need to keep their bodies in good shape. The topic of health receives a good deal of attention today. Information on healthy diets, regular exercise, and unloading stress can be found in most popular magazines. Fitness centers have sprung up throughout most metropolitan centers. The media frequently advertises memberships to these centers or fitness

19

equipment that can be used at home. Why, then, aren't more people using these tremendous tools and becoming more physically fit? Why is high blood pressure and other heart-related diseases on the increase? We driven Americans are beginning to learn what many people in other places in the world have already learned: A healthy life requires a proper balance of nutrition, exercise, and leisure. Unless careful attention is paid, the balance can be easily upset and not so easily restored.

God's people who want to enjoy good health know they must take care of their bodies, caring for them as we honor God's Son who bought us from sin, death, and the devil, paying for us with His life. Paul reminds us, "You are not your own; you were bought at a price. Therefore honor God with your body" (1 Corinthians 6:19–20).

React and Respond

1. What does work mean to you?

2. Talk about the place of stress in your life. Where does it come from? What do you do about it? How often do you feel helpless around stress?

3. What is your favorite form of exercise or recreation?

4. Consider the following verses: "Everyone who competes in the games goes into strict training. They do it to get a crown that will not last; but we do it to get a crown that will

last forever. Therefore I do not run like a man running aimlessly; I do not fight like a man beating the air. No, I beat my body and make it my slave so that after I have preached to others, I myself will not be disqualified for the prize" (1 Corinthians 9:25–26). What kind of strict training do you undergo in order to keep your body in submission? For what benefit? What happens when the Spirit of God who lives within you is in control of your life?

5. What does it mean to you to have been bought with a price? How do you worship God in the care you provide for His temple—your body?

Let's Get Moving!

God has put our bodies together in a marvelous manner. The psalmist declares, "I praise You because I am fearfully and wonderfully made. ... When I was woven together in the depths of the earth, Your eyes saw my unformed body" (Psalm 139:14–15).

In our desire to honor God with our proper care of the body He has given to each of us, we must include a plan to get into shape.

Whichever exercise method you chose, prepare by seeing a doctor before beginning exercise and regularly while in training. Learn what range of motion you can expect for your age, size/weight, and health condition. Learn how to prepare yourself by stretching and breathing before you exercise. And if preparation is important, so is cooling down after. Many professional athletes know the value of training during the off season and of easing away from strenuous activity rather than abruptly stopping. Learn dietary information about

21

which fuel is most appropriate for a variety of activities and purposes.

Think about how God has also encouraged moderation by setting a pattern of six days of work and a day of Sabbath.

React and Respond

1. How often do you exercise?

2. When is the last time you had a thorough physical? How closely have you followed the recommendations of your doctors in terms of diet, exercise, and weight control?

3. Sweating is often understood as a part of God's curse upon Adam and Eve (Genesis 3:19). Reflect on the positive and negative aspects of sweating. What part does it have in your life?

Bodily Care in Perspective

For some people exercise is a process they use to become fit. Others seem to make their exercise an end in itself. They worship the body rather than the God who made it. Paul warns that some people have "exchanged the truth of God for a lie, and worshiped and served created things rather than the Creator" (Romans 1:25).

Like many things in life, moderation is a recommended path to follow. There is a delicate balance between becoming physically fit to be able to function better and live longer and actually idolizing a fit body.

Within the past decade more and more people have taken up running as a method of exercise. Some describe what they call the "runner's high." They pass a certain point where pain no longer accompanies their exertion. They actually feel a "high." They are energized by their effort. Others have come to learn that running takes more exertion than is safe for them. Walking, however, can be done by people of all ages. Others add more competition and companionship to their exercise regiment by choosing golf or tennis as their preferred exercise. The key is to do something that you enjoy so you will stay with it.

React and Respond

1. When can the care and performance of our bodies receive too much attention in the life of the Christian?

2. At what point do you think exercise becomes an end in itself instead of a means to stay fit? How would you tell if you were at that point?

3. What type of physical activity is best for you?

Running to Win

In 1 Corinthians 6:19 Paul asks, "Do you not know that your body is a temple of the Holy Spirit?" In Paul's day there were many large temples in the cities and countryside through which he traveled. When Paul compared the human body to a temple of the living God, he was encouraging proper respect and care for it, reminding the people that by faith they carried the living God around with them in their appearance, in their actions, and in the words they spoke and the attitudes they projected.

In 1 Corinthians 9:24 Paul writes, "Do you know that in a race all the runners run, but only one gets the prize? Run in such a way as to get the prize."

Paul encourages us to "run to win"—to rely on the Spirit's power to live each day for Him who died for us and rose again. Consider the urgency and intensity with which Jesus approached life. He came into life with the single-minded purpose to save people. He went about doing good, preaching forgiveness and peace to people burdened with guilt and despair. He forgave sins, upsetting the religious establishment of His day. As opposition from religious leaders increased, it became apparent that they could no longer tolerate the strength and clear focus of Jesus' life. They crucified Him, thinking it was the end of His words and deeds. In truth it was the goal of His ministry. "For even the Son of Man did not come to be served, but to serve, and to give His life as a ransom for many" (Mark 10:45).

Do you have a similar focus on what is important in your life? How have you prioritized your work and leisure?

React and Respond

1. Who is this Holy Spirit whom Paul says lives in the temple of your body? (See 1 Corinthians 6:11.)

2. As you live the Christian life, how can others tell when you are "running to win" and when you aren't? Which areas of your life currently require the greatest amount of your energy? Explain.

3. For years the United States Army has attracted recruits with the motto "Be all you can be!" In the space below, write down what you like about your body and what you don't you like about your body. Which list is longer? Why?

4. A well-known and simple truth says, "A journey of a thousand miles begins with the first step." If you could change one thing about the way you exercise right now, what would it be? Why don't you change it now?

3 Living a Balanced Life

A Look at a Life

God has given us all we are and have. He has blessed us with a beautiful world and surrounds us with people to love and material things to bring comfort and meaning to our existence. Unfortunately, in our preoccupation with ourselves and daily concerns we often forget our reason for being—to glorify God and help His people. We take God and the good things He has given us for granted. Consider the following reflections of an older adult.

If I had my life to live over, I'd try to make more mistakes next time. I would relax. I would limber up. I would be sillier than I have been this trip. I know of very few things I would take seriously. I would be crazier. I would be less hygienic. I would climb more mountains, swim more rivers, and watch more sunsets. I would burn more gasoline. I would eat more ice cream and less beans. I would have more actual troubles and fewer imaginary ones. You see I am one of those people who lives life prophetically and sensibly and sanely, hour after hour, day after day. Oh, I have had my moments, and, if I had it to do over again, I'd have more of them. In fact, I'd try to have nothing else. Just moment after moment, one after the other, instead of living so many years ahead each day. I have been one of those people who never go anywhere without a thermometer, a hot water bottle, a gargle, a raincoat, and a parachute. If I had it to do over again, I would go places and do things and travel lighter than I have. If I had my life to do over, I would start barefooted earlier in the spring and stay that way later in the fall. I would play hooky more. I wouldn't make such good grades except by accident. I would ride on more merry-go-rounds. I would pick more daisies!

Nadine Stair

React and Respond

1. What point is the author of the preceding quotation making? Do you agree or disagree with his perspective?

2. Think back on your life and the priorities you have adopted for yourself. What things would you do differently, if you could begin your life over again?

Rest and Rust!

A kindergartner once quipped, "Resting is a waste of time!" On old-timer on the job, in an attempt to use guilt to motivate a new employee into working harder, sternly told him, "If you rest, you'll rust!" These comments may lead us to wonder whether the world is made up of two different kinds of people: those who value staying busy all the time and those who appear to be lazy.

Good machinery is made to work. Actually, a well-built machine is better off if it is kept working than if it just sits around idle from time to time. But the human body is more than a marvelous machine. Our bodies are creations of a loving God, designed and built to give Him praise and glory. And we cannot adequately praise God if we are broken down or tired.

React and Respond

1. In the *Wizard of Oz*, the Tim Man rusted not because he rested but because he didn't oil himself thoroughly during a rainstorm. Some people work hard physically all day and want nothing more than to rest and relax after work. They

would rather do anything than "work" longer hours at home. They need a change of pace for their bodies and their minds. What is the "oil" that keeps your body in shape?

2. Some men have a well-oiled exercise routine which they repeat often and regularly to keep their bodies functioning smoothly. Others, sensing a need, exercise vigorously for a while but soon taper off and eventually quit exercising altogether. Make a seven-column chart of your week. Let each column represent the 24 hours you have each day, and mark the times of the day along the left side of your chart. Draw vertical lines representing those hours spent sleeping and those at work each day. Now figure out how much time you spend in preparation for bed, for work, for meals, and any other preparation you do. Figure the time you spend in prayer and in the study of God's Word and the amount of time you spend in recreation and exercise. What's left over?

What changes would you like to make? Why?

3. What is your perspective on work and rest. Are you the type of person who finds himself saying, "I just don't have the time?" Or, do you find yourself often wondering what to do next? Are you at your best when you have several projects or books going at once, or do you prefer to start a new project only after you have completed the last?

4. It has been said that "one machine can do the work of 50 ordinary men. But no machine can do the work of one extraordinary man." React to this comment.

5. Sidney Harris once said, "The real danger is not that computers will begin to think like men but that men will begin to think like computers." Explain.

Rest Is Repair

When a ship is brought in for repairs, it is often put onto a "dry dock," which means that it is lifted out of its normal place in the water so the repairs can be made away from its usual environment—water. When an automobile is in for repairs, we say it is "in the shop." Men too need periodic "time out" for bodily repair and rejuvenation. Some men avoid regular and routine checkups; visiting the doctor just isn't the macho thing to do. It's hard to imagine Rambo or the high-plains drifter expressing concern about missing an annual physical or six-month checkup at the dentist's office.

But as men, we need to be concerned about our health. When warning signs signal that something may be wrong, we need to see a doctor immediately. And we need regularly to take time out to rest. As Daniel Josselyn put it, "Rest is not a matter of doing absolutely nothing. Rest is repair!"

Many people joke about being in a rat race, but few people are willing to do anything about it. Few are willing to say no to more and more work, with less and less time for rest in between. People rush home from work to relax briefly before they go somewhere else. How true is Lewis Carroll's quote from *Through the Looking Glass*, "It takes all the running you can do to keep in the same place. If you want to get somewhere else, you must run at least twice as fast."

Consider God's wisdom. He rested on the seventh day. In so doing He told us to set aside a time to allow our bodies to repair themselves so that they might be well equipped to face the stresses and challenges of the work days. Of greater importance, He reminds us to take time for the rest and refreshing our soul needs and finds through spending time in God's Word. We can spend time in the Word in private, with our families, and together with those with whom we assemble to hear God's Word spoken and explained, to sing it in praise, pray according to it, and receive it at the Lord's Table together with bread and the fruit of the vine.

REACT and RESPOND

1. If you have ever worked nonstop for a great length of time, how did you feel about rest?

2. What is the difference between your body and a machine?

3. On a scale of 1 (very poorly) to 10 (very well), how well are you doing at maintaining a healthy balance in your life between work and rest?

Our Daily Bread

In creating all that exists, God used unseen building materials to call into existence that which is seen. The writer to the Hebrews declares, "By faith we understand that the universe was formed at God's command, so that what is seen was not made out of what was visible" (Hebrews 11:3). And then God rested. In resting on the seventh day, God was creating an intentional pattern or cycle for us to follow: Work for six days and rest on the seventh. As we have explored earlier, this cycle of work and rest was further broken down by God's people. They knew they could only work a portion of each day so they rested when the sun did. God further defined rest by declaring a Sabbath for the land, directing the people to allowing their land to lie fallow or dormant one year out of each seven. Even in the cycle of seedtime and harvest, God is providing a model for work and rest that is vital to life and health.

When the well-oiled machinery of your body rests, it repairs and recuperates. Cells take on energy from the carbohydrates and sugars which you consume. Your cells also use the building blocks of protein to repair and rejuvenate themselves. God made everything about you to work together in a beautiful concert of work and rest, relaxation and rejuvenation. Our minds and hearts listen to God as He encourages us to maintain this precious balance.

While wandering in the wilderness, God taught His people a very important lesson about "daily bread," (Matthew 6:11). God promised a daily rain of bread, called manna, for His hungry people. "Then the LORD said to Moses, 'I will rain down bread from heaven for you. The people are to go out each day and gather enough for that day. In this way I will test them and see whether they will follow My instructions. On the sixth day they are to prepare what they bring in, and that is to be twice as much as they gather on the other days' " (Exodus 16:4–5).

Some greedily tried to gather up more than they needed only to discover that the food they hoarded quickly spoiled (Exodus 16:16–20). When God's people in Moses' time grumbled and complained about the lack of variety in their diet, God supplemented the morning rain of bread with an evening flock of quail, just sufficient for their daily meat require-ments. And so they traveled through the wilderness, heading for a "land flowing with milk and honey" (Exodus 3:8).

God wants us to recognize our dependency on Him. "Your strength will equal your days" (Deuteronomy 33:25). When we pray the prayer our Lord taught us, we acknowledge that God gives us bread and the strength to gather it each day. We ask that He would continue to give us all that we need to sustain ourselves and to share with others.

React and Respond

1. How do you maintain a balance between work and rest in your life? Share your plan with someone else.

2. Why do you think God blessed the "seventh day" as a day of rest?

3. Think about the words *balance* and *intentional* as they describe your work/rest cycle. What happens when this cycle gets out of balance? What happens when you are less intentional or deliberate about either rest or work?

4. What "daily bread" is most important to you today? Why? Confess your gratefulness to God and to one other person.

5. Why do you think God allowed His people to gather a double portion of manna only on the sixth day? What lesson do you find here about timing and pacing?

Life Patterns

In some families fathers teach the children the value of work by allowing it to consume them. They arrive at work early and return home from work late, bringing a healthy portion of their work home with them. In other families, fathers clearly divide their profession from their life at home. They leave to go to work and arrive back home according to a schedule from which they seldom if ever deviate. Their time at home is dedicated to the family and to the home. Family vacations and other outings are a regular part of the family routine.

Drs. Murry Bowen and Edwin Friedmann have pioneered the family system theory which suggests that what we learn growing up in our homes we tend to replicate in our homes, our jobs, and our churches, and other social institutions. We then perpetuate these in the other families we join. Rabbi Edwin H. Friedmann, in his highly popular *Generation to Generation: Natural Process and Family Systems in Church and Synagogue,* says, "Because the emotional process in all of these systems is identical, unresolved issues in any one of them can produce symptoms in the others, and increased understanding of any one creates more effective functioning in all three." To state it in another way, "The apple doesn't fall far from the tree."

Who plans your agenda? Who writes your scripts? Quite possibly your parents, grandparents, and the leaders of the churches and other social institutions to which you and your family have belonged. You may have never thought about it before, but others have played an important part in writing your life's script. Now you must decide how you will play it out.

React and Respond

1. Who has been most instrumental in teaching you a "work ethic"? Whom have you helped to form a work ethic of his or her own and how?

2. How do you provide intentional leadership for others in the area of rest and recreation?

Lighten Up!

When fast food restaurants first opened several decades ago, they didn't open their doors for the day until just before the lunch hour. Most stayed open only until shortly after the supper hour. Gradually they lengthened their hours into the evenings, knowing that some people would eat after a movie or social event. Then someone got the bright idea that most restaurants contained all that was necessary to increase their productivity by a third if they opened earlier and added breakfast items to their menu. Many fast food restaurants are now open 24 hours a day.

Today, Americans have extended the amount of time and energy they devote to work in quest for more of the things money will buy. Some have taken on a second and third job. Few homes today exist on a single income. Many families find themselves with an ever-diminishing amount of time to play together. Laughter in the family has been replaced with increased stress.

Bridges have safe load limits. When the limit on a bridge is exceeded, it may bear the overload for a short time but soon will bend and even break with only a small increase in weight. When the safe load limit of a vehicle is exceeded, it may bear the extra overload for a brief time, but the load will take its toll. God has also designed our bodies for specific limits. Over time we learn that these limits may be exceeded—only slightly, and from time to time. We can lift and carry heavy—and at times even heroic—amounts. But sooner or later our bodies will break.

Bridges are often built with a specific upward curve. This tension helps the bridge bear a greater than expected load. Bridges are actually stronger under a moderate load due to the distribution of stresses along each of the members of the bridge. But a bow, bent for too long, may never return to its original shape. We can not constantly work our bodies beyond the limit without lasting negative results.

The apostle Paul continually emphasizes that the church, the fellowship of the people of God is a community—a group of people bound together by our common faith in much the same way as a family is bound together by name, identity, and affiliation. In Galatians 6 he encourages believers to "carry each other's burdens, and in this way you will fulfill the law of Christ" (v. 2). A few verses later he also reminds his fellow Christians, "Each one should carry his own load" (v. 5).

Paul's words indicate that normally burdens ought to be borne by the individual on whom they fall as a matter of personal responsibility. But when it becomes an overload—a particularly burdensome and exhausting hardship—then other Christians can and will help to shoulder the load. Even with all the work the pioneers of this country had to do, they understood that when many people gathered together for a barn raising or to help someone who was sick complete their harvest, the work went easier. It was more fun too! Many willing hands always seem to make a task enjoyable.

Jesus showed the way for us when it comes to burden-bearing. To free us and all people from the devil's power, Jesus took our burden upon Himself and suffered, died, and rose again in our place. On the cross, He paid the price for our sins and eased the burden of guilt, shame, and loneliness which we all bear since the fall into sin in the Garden. Because of Jesus, God offers us forgiveness—fully and completely. With His forgiveness we are continually empowered to begin life anew with the slate wiped clean, planning and adopting a new plan to give glory to God and more positive attention to ourselves and all those whose lives we touch.

We do ourselves a favor, both individually and as members of a family and a larger community, when we plan regular, balanced, and intentional times of rest and recreation so that the tension can be relieved and, if possible, rechanneled from time to time.

React and Respond

1. How do you know when your load has become an overload? What do you do about it?

2. How has Christ lightened your burden? What difference does this make in your daily life?

3. How do others know that your burdens have been shared and lightened?

4. What does forgiveness mean to you? How does forgiveness lighten the load of your brothers in the faith?

Healthy Hobbies 4

"Get a Life!"

High school sweethearts Sam and Molly married just after Sam graduated from the university and landed his first full-time job. They moved around the country as Sam advanced in his career, raising their children, building a nest egg for their retirement. Molly had worked only part-time on evenings and weekends so one of them could always be home with the kids. Some time after their last child started school, Molly began to daydream about finishing college since she had completed only two years of school.

Because the local university offered an evening and weekend college completion program, Molly was able to keep her part-time job while she finished school. After a year and a half, she graduated with high honors and immediately landed a job in industrial technology. Molly was happy.

But as Sam began to think about early retirement, he realized that with Molly's new career, they would not be able to travel together as he once had dreamed. Molly would now be out of town on business trips a good bit of the time. Sam soon found himself at home alone many evenings and some weekends. When he protested, she reminded him of all the time he had spent on the road during the early years of his career. She jokingly responded to his nagging by saying one day, "Sam, why don't you get a life!"

Sam was stunned. They had always planned things together, but now it seemed that separate careers had driven a wedge between them. Sam found himself dreading each night he spent alone. Although hurt by her words, he realized that he didn't have a hobby or outside interest. Molly had always been the one to plan their vacations and keep their social calendar. Sam depended on her for more than he realized.

Suddenly, early retirement didn't hold the attraction it

had once held for him. Sam began to think about what he would do while Molly, who had begun her career later in life, completed her time until her retirement at age 65. He knew that his life would change when he retired, but what about Molly's? How would her life change if she retired? And if he dreaded an empty evening now, what would every day seem like after he retired and Molly was still working?

Sam began to do some serious thinking about the intensity with which he had entered his career. He discovered that Molly's suggestion to "get a life," although half in jest, was worth consideration. Sam needed outside interests. He needed a hobby.

At age 50 Sam set out to find a hobby. He began to search his memory for things that he had done while younger. Most of the things he came up with now seemed empty and childish. His job and family had been his whole life. Sam became severely depressed. Finally, he sought the help of a counselor.

React and Respond

1. What do you think the counselor told Sam? What would you tell Sam if you were his friend?

2. In what ways are hobbies planning for retirement? How well planned is your retirement? Why do many people fail to become involved in activities that they can carry with them into maturity?

3. What would you suggest to the 50-year-old who wants to participate in sumo wrestling as a hobby? What makes a hobby healthy? When can a hobby become unhealthy?

Who Are You?

> O LORD, You have searched me and You know me. You
> know when I sit and when I rise; You perceive my thoughts
> from afar. Psalm 139:1–2

Do you know who you are? The psalmist says that God knows you inside and out—even better than you know yourself. If you just met someone and wanted to get to know him better, you would come up with ways to spend time with him. Think about your relationship with yourself. What do you do to get to know yourself better? Most of us are so busy with the demands of life that we have little time to think about ourselves, about ourselves and our relationship with God, about ourselves and our relationship with others.

From God's Word we know that Jesus joined those around Him in celebrations and other activities usually associated with leisure time. Jesus periodically went away to talk with God in prayer (e.g., Mark 1:35). We know that He attended a wedding with His family and friends (John 2:1–11), and He ate and drank with others (Matthew 11:18–19).

God wants us to enjoy this life, since it is really the beginning of eternity. Jesus said, "I have come that they may have life, and have it to the full" (John 10:10). Jesus earned full life for us by living a perfect life, suffering and dying at Calvary, and rising in victory over death on the third day. Because of Him we have eternal life—an unending and perfectly satisfying existence that became our legacy the moment we came to faith.

Film producer Quincy Jones, after surviving a brain aneurism and two serious brain surgeries, said, "God has given each one of us approximately 25,000 days on this earth. I truly believe that He has something very specific in mind—8,300 to sleep, 8,300 to work, and 8,300 to give, live, play, pray, and love one another." No matter how busy Jones becomes, he always makes sure that there is time in his schedule for fun.

React and Respond

1. Who are you? Does your work define you? Does your sense of humor and adventure define who you are? Explain.

2. Big changes are the most difficult to make. What changes could you make in your life right now to help you to get to know yourself better?

3. Make a list of all the activities you enjoy. Next, add those hobbies or leisure pursuits of which you are aware that others enjoy. Finally, do some research about hobbies, perhaps in a library or on the World Wide Web under leisure or hobby. Did you gain any further insights about what you would enjoy doing for fun?

The Origin of Interests

The dictionary defines a hobby as something people do in their spare or free time. Many people develop hobbies which are completely different from their professions: a brain surgeon enjoys auto racing and demolition derbies; a garbage collector collects and mounts butterflies. Most often, though, selection of any particular interest or hobby is rooted in some unspoken lessons conveyed by parents.

In general, fathers make a lasting impression on their children by what they do rather than by what they say. And how they choose to spend their free time is probably just as important for their children as what they have chosen as their life's vocation. Someone once said that children are like wet cement—whatever falls on them makes an impression.

In our lives we often prove true the old adage "Like father like son." We tend to adopt many of the habits—good and bad—of our parents. Children must make careful decisions about how they will spend their time because habits developed early are difficult to break. Parents do their children a good service by helping them to make healthy decisions about not only how they work but also about how they play and otherwise use their leisure time.

Throughout life, hobbies can bring fathers and children together. Those bonded together in families often find themselves sharing similar interests and inclinations. One young boy learned to enjoy a hobby early in life. He begged and pleaded with his father to join him in the hobby, but the father never seemed to have the time. Finally, in retirement, the father surprised his now-grown son by finally joining him in the hobby.

When today's parents get home from work, they must still spend time preparing food, cleaning, and maintaining their home. Most children live within a two-income family, but many also have parents living in separate households, each with his or her home to maintain. For those of us who are parents, time is at a premium so we must be very careful in making decisions about how we will spend what little of the time we have left to ourselves. Leisure time is that which is left over after all the other obligations are met.

Some people get involved in hobbies only to learn that they require an assortment of equipment and resources. Many people will say they don't have a hobby because they don't have the time. Actually everyone has the same amount of time—each person just chooses to use it in his own way.

One man went to the store to buy a backyard jungle gym for his children. He found the one they liked and was at the point of purchasing it when he happened to read a notice on the box. Because over 1,000 nuts and bolts were required to assemble the toy, the instructions suggested that for safety's sake the tightness of each should be checked at least once each month. To the deep disappointment of his children, he left the store without purchasing the jungle gym. "If I spend only 10 seconds on each bolt each month I'll have to commit more than an hour and half a month to maintaining it. I don't want to invest that kind of time in a toy."

While we all have the same amount of time, people make decisions about how much time they will spend in various endeavors. In life, like many organizations, there will be those who will be very involved, and some who just want to remain on the edge. Some will run for office; others will want to maintain membership, without ever holding an official position. I remember reading about a sailing club in which a third of the people owned and sailed their boats, another third owned but never sailed their boats, and the final third neither owned nor sailed in boats. Although all belonged to the club, some sailed and others found their enjoyment in talking about sailing. Due to individual differences, those who share an interest may express their interest in a variety of ways.

React and Respond

1. Think of significant, positive role models in your life. What examples do they provide for you in their management of work, fun, and recreation?

2. What hobbies did your mother, father, and/or grandparents have? How could you learn more about them and what they did for fun? What clues does this provide for you in your understanding of your use of leisure?

3. What factors affect your interest in activities during your free time (e.g., cost, who else is involved, curiosity, intrigue, convenience)?

Hobbies and Pastimes in Modern Times

Many hardworking people of long ago would have ridiculed expenditures of time and money on hobbies. Such expenses would have been considered frivolous. The simpler, more common games, toys, and hobbies enjoyed by most people were homemade usually of materials close at hand and inexpensive. In a time when the primary activities of life were work and sleep, fun and play were especially important. Recreation often meant lavish celebrations, including meals and noncompetitive games.

In modern times, games, play, and hobbies make a significant contribution to the economy. Certain areas of our country that formerly had agricultural or industrial-based economies have changed completely. Many now list tourism and recreation as their major sources of income. Hobbies, sporting activities, and travel have become multibillion dollar industries.

Even people in extreme northern portions of our country have discovered ways to enjoy the outdoors all year round. The winter weekend exodus to the lake or country retreat nearly rivals that of the summer in many areas of the country. Once recreationists waited patiently for the three or four months of more temperate weather in the summer. Now they are finding activities that make for year-round fun. Some are willing to spend thousands of dollars on recreation.

Ancient writers sometimes referred to human beings as "homo ludens"—the one who plays. Play is the "work" of children, but people of all ages benefit from play. The renewal and rejuvenation that come from and with play are beneficial to physical and mental health.

God has given us the gift of our bodies. He has also given many things around us to enjoy. Work is important in defining ourselves, but so is play. Work is important in providing income and keeping our physical bodies together. But play is important too, both for the physical exercise it often provides and for the mental shifting of gears that promotes good emotional health.

The play we choose as children is an important determiner in the play we will engage in as adults. Some hobbies may be very expensive but require almost no physical activity. We will want to maintain a balance with hobbies that provide exercise and which are available to anyone, regardless of financial resources.

God has richly gifted us to live in a time and place where we have multiple opportunities for play. May we seek to use the resources He has given us wisely—to enjoy hobbies which both entertain and help us maintain health.

REACT OR RESPOND

1."Play is the work of a child." Describe to someone how you are different at play than at work.

2. Consider God's word from Exodus 33:14, "My Presence will go with you, and I will give you rest." How do you notice that God's presence is different when you are playing than when you are working? than when you were a child?

3. "All work and no play make Jack a very dull boy." What about Jack is dull when he doesn't play? How have you ever noticed this happening to you or someone you know?

LET'S GO FISHING

One of the more popular recreational pastimes is fishing. Millions fish and for a variety of reasons. Some fish for sport and release what they catch. Some seek the biggest fish, always looking for a record catch. Others fish to eat but end up releasing most of their catch. Jesus' disciples had been fishermen before they became disciples; they caught and sold fish to make a living.

Shortly after Jesus rose from the dead, He met one of the women who had been close to Him. He gave her these instructions. "Go and tell My brothers to go to Galilee; there they will see Me" (Matthew 28:10). The disciples then traveled north—to Galilee. St. John relates that one day Peter abruptly announced, "I'm going out to fish." The other disciples promptly joined him. After a long night, during which they caught nothing, Jesus appeared on the shore. From a distance He asked, "Friends, haven't you any fish?" Then He told them to let down their nets on the right side of their boat. The disciples caught so many fish that their nets were beginning to break.

Several of the disciples had grown up around the Sea of Galilee. They knew about boats and fishing. Did this event remind Peter of a lesson Jesus taught when He called Peter and his companions to become fishers of men (Luke 5:1–11), or did it remind Peter of the time that the Lord approached the disciples' boat one night out on the stormy sea (Matthew 14:22–33)? Or, did Peter remember another lesson of faith when a sudden storm on the lake caused him to fear for his life even though Jesus was aboard (Luke 8:22–25)?

The resurrected Jesus used this occasion by the Sea of Galilee to teach them another great lesson of faith. It centered around the centuries-old practice of fishing. Just at the point when His followers were frustrated and disappointed, Jesus knew exactly where they could find what they sought (John 21:1–14).

Have you ever gone fishing? Why did you go? Did you seek fish, fun, or frustration? If you have ever fished, no doubt you've experienced all three. But many people say they fish because of the relaxation it offers. They are away from job, office, phone, and many other distractions. They are not in control—God and the fish are! Like so many other hobbies and recreational activities, fishing provides a much needed change of pace from the stress-filled, nonstop action of the work day.

God has provided many opportunities, such as fishing, in which we can rest, relax, recharge, and shift gears so that we will be invigorated and ready for work after a break. Fishing, for many men, is a gift from God. We can sit and do absolutely nothing—and still look busy.

Perhaps like Peter, we can use fishing as an excuse to get away— from the harsh realities of a busy work schedule, or the stress of making decisions and helping others do the same. God is so good. He has given us oceans, lakes, and streams. He created fish to fill them. And He created us to enjoy all these simple pleasures.

Perhaps fishing is not your choice for a hobby. Perhaps you would rather do anything else than fish. What then would it be? Would you rather read, whitewater raft, or climb a mountain? Would you sooner cut bait than fish? No matter. Just as long as its different from what you normally do to earn a paycheck. And just as long as you find it fun, enjoyable, and rewarding.

How do you feel when you are engaged in your hobby? Do you believe that God is glorified whenever you enjoy yourself? And do you believe that God's name is praised whenever one of His creatures enjoys His creation in a way that He intended? Then join Peter in saying "Let's go fishing!"

React and Respond

1. Jesus knows all things. Why do you think Jesus asked His disciples, "Have you any fish?"

2. When do you get away from it all? What provides you the opportunity to shift gears?

3. Do you ever feel guilty when you relax? How can you learn to be more comfortable while taking a break?

4. Write a few statements about why you believe it is important to depend on Jesus for everything. Now share your thoughts with another person. What does it mean to have faith in Jesus for everything?

5. Suppose your plans for being with others for this evening or weekend were suddenly canceled. Would you look forward to an evening alone, or would you dread it? Why?

6. Consider everything you've read and said about hobbies to this point in the chapter. Can any hobby become a time-robber? How can you create boundaries around and set limits on any hobby activity?

5 | Addictive Behaviors: Misuses of Leisure Time

The Crazy Man Driving My Bus!

One night I had a dream. I saw many of the foolish things I had done in my life. I watched myself rushing around, making careless errors, doing things just to be doing them, and not really paying attention to what was going on around me or what was happening to me. Then I dreamed that there was a little trap door in my forehead. I reached up and opened it and looked into a mirror to see what was behind the little trap door. There was a little man inside, dressed in a blue bus driver's suit. He had a steering wheel grasped firmly in his hands. I realized then the man was driving my bus! This little, crazy man was driving my life! Who is that man? C'est moi! It is I!

If you have ever felt that your life was out of control, then you can begin to understand the craziness that accompanies what is often called compulsive behavior. Compulsive behavior includes things which people continue to do, not understanding why they are doing them. They continue a particular behavior regardless of the harm it brings upon themselves or others. Some habits are potentially harmful: excessive drinking, smoking, or eating. Yet people can be compulsive about positive activities, such as recreation, exercise, and even sexuality. Just as we can overdo hobbies or relationships, we also can become addicted to just about anything.

The key to recovery lies in understanding ourselves and why we are doing what we are doing. Much of why we do what we do originates within our family of origin. While others help to provide our basic life patterns, each individual acts on them in his own way. Each individual is the crazy person driving the bus of his life.

Pause, for a moment, to consider some of the forces that are squeezing the life out of our leisure time. Studies suggest that one in ten people in the United States is addicted to some form of a mood-altering chemical. The most popular, because it is the most affordable and accessible, is alcohol. A number of years ago, the American Medical Association passed a controversial resolution, stating that chemical addiction is a disease. The decision sparked a lively debate, at times almost a battle.

Religious leaders objected that drunkenness is a personal sin. Some medical researches and practitioners protested that alcoholism doesn't meet the classical criteria of disease—that is, an invasion of some foreign agent into the body. And while many psychologists were in agreement with the resolution, they wondered where the new classification would ultimately lead to in medical diagnosis and treatment.

In defending its decision, the AMA reported that it made this dramatic move for several reasons. The AMA wanted people to understand that chemical dependency is treatable—as a disease. This decision also allowed health insurance companies to cover the treatment of alcoholism. They were very quick to add that there is, in fact, no cure for alcoholism and chemical addiction. However, with proper understanding and help, individuals can begin a lifelong process of recovery.

Some compulsive behaviors, such as drinking, drug abuse, compulsive gambling, and overeating, are strongly connected to leisure. People become addicted to the *pleasure* they experience in using these substances. But other compulsive behaviors are very much part of our working life. Some people become addicted to work; they become "hooked" on the pleasure and the process of doing satisfying things over and over. Workaholism is like being stuck in the mud and spinning your tires. You work hard, but don't go anywhere. Yet you enjoy stepping on the gas pedal, rocking back and forth, and even planning your next move.

In order to maintain a healthy life, and especially leisure time, we want to minimize—if not eliminate—unhealthy, dangerous behavior. Fortunately, we have a loving and gracious God who cares about every aspect of our lives. His power is always available to help us to become the best we can be.

React and Respond

1. When have you felt out of control in life? What did you do?

2. How do you feel about alcoholism classified as a disease? Do you agree or disagree with the AMA? Why?

3. How can God help you when you feel out of control (see 1 Peter 5:7)? How does the power of Christ's forgiveness set you free to enjoy your leisure?

Addiction: Denial of Powerlessness

Do you know what an addiction is? Anne Wilson Schaef and Diane Fassel of The Addictive Organization define addiction as "any substance or process that has taken over our lives and over which we are powerless."

People may be addicted to a substance such as alcohol or a drug, or to a process, such as work, gambling, or sexual activity. The pleasure they gain from compulsively repeating the activity seems to outweigh the pain that results when they do it over and over again. Pleasure from repetition is more important than the pain which causes them to do it in the first place.

Most people agree with the statement that "once an

addict always an addict." There really is no cure for addiction—only a process called recovery, which, once begun, lasts forever. Many experts agree that addictions seldom come alone; addictive behaviors like company. People who are addicted to one substance or process are usually compulsive about something else, even though the abuse may not immediately be as evident. Since the most popular and well-known addiction is to alcohol, whatever is true about this addiction is probably true about many, if not all others.

A world-famous book officially titled *Alcoholics Anonymous*, and unofficially and affectionately known as *The Big Book*, contains the story of how thousands of men and women have begun to recover from alcoholism.

In this book Bill W. tells his story of decline from casual to serious drinking. At first he enjoyed a drink of alcohol. Later he knew that he needed a drink. Soon he was begging for a drink. He finally stooped to lying and even stealing to get a drink. He came to realize that alcohol was his master and that he could not stop drinking by himself. He had always believed in some kind of Higher Power, greater than himself, who was able to help him. But he had never really surrendered himself to this Higher Power. Finally, when he could go no further and it appeared that he had come to the end of his resources, Bill W. asked for help.

Bill W., a New York stockbroker, realized that his life was completely unmanageable. He could not control his urge to drink to excess. He kept repeating behavior that he knew, when sober, to be destructive and even life-threatening. Suddenly, he had a "religious experience" which transformed his life and eventually that of millions. Bill W. yielded his life to God—to his Higher Power.

Bill W. also firmly believed that only one alcoholic could help another alcoholic. One day, while on a business trip to Akron, Ohio, he was near collapse. He had not taken a drink for some time and was strongly tempted to start drinking again. At just that moment he met another alcoholic, the man who would later become the co-founder of AA. Dr. Bob was also addicted to alcohol.

Together they shared their experiences and their hopelessness. They both had a desire to help someone else, and so they did. They helped each other and founded a group which has touched more people than any other nonreligious organization in the world to date. It was June 10, 1935. Neither ever took another drop of alcohol again.

Bill W. and Dr. Bob set out to help others, and soon their numbers grew. They desired to remain anonymous, and therefore used only first names and last initials. AA meetings began to spring up in public and private buildings throughout the country. One of the trademarks of these meetings was that they were informal and self-led. Because everyone agreed to be anonymous, recovering alcoholics found they can honestly bare their souls with no fear of breach of privacy. The success of the group is due in large part to the belief that only an alcoholic can help another alcoholic.

Another important and well-known mark of these groups is the use of the Serenity Prayer: "God grant me the serenity to accept the things I cannot change, courage to change the things I can, and the wisdom to know the difference! Amen."

Within just a few short years, groups around the country had heard of the success of AA in helping others to quit drinking. Many began to use the Akron group's ideas. Men and women began to discover the kind of support that was needed to get and remain sober. Up to that point, no other group or treatment process had been as successful in helping people recover from their addictions.

Bill W. and Dr. Bob developed the Twelve Steps of AA— an outline that describes the process of recovery from addiction to alcohol. In recent years, the Twelve Steps have been borrowed and modified, but never improved upon. Alcoholics believe they are never cured and will in fact never be able to drink alcohol again. These steps lead an alcoholic through a process of recovery which once begun is never ended.

The Twelve steps of Alcoholics Anonymous are as follows:
1. We admitted we were powerless over alcohol—that our lives had become unmanageable.
2. Came to believe that a Power greater than ourselves could restore us to sanity.
3. Made a decision to turn our will and our lives over to the care of God *as we understood Him.*
4. Make a searching and fearless moral inventory of ourselves.

5. Admitted to God, to ourselves and to another human being the exact nature of our wrongs.
6. Were entirely ready to have God remove all these defects of character.
7. Humbly asked Him to remove our shortcomings.
8. Made a list of all persons we had harmed, and became willing to make amends to them all.
9. Made direct amends to such people wherever possible, except when to do so would injure them or others.
10. Continued to take personal inventory and when we were wrong promptly admitted it.
11. Sought through prayer and meditation to improve our conscious contact with God, *as we understood Him*, praying only for knowledge of His will for us and the power to carry that out.
12. Having had a spiritual awakening as the result of these steps, we tried to carry this message to alcoholics, and to practice these principles in all our affairs.

Thousands of AA groups meet weekly in most cities in the United States. In larger cities, there are countless AA groups meeting each day in a number of convenient locations throughout the city. The location of a nearby AA group can be obtained by dialing a phone number listed in many telephone directories under "Alcoholics Anonymous." In smaller communities, the location of an AA group is often not a well-kept secret, but the identify of those who attend and what is discussed at the meetings are.

Another group, called Al-anon is for friends and family members of alcoholics. Al-ateen is for teenage friends and family members. These groups provide support for people who are known as co-dependent.

Alcoholism is often called a family disease: If one member of a family is afflicted, others will often get sick too. Often these secondary or supporting groups conveniently meet at the same time and in the same location as AA groups. But they always hold separate meetings and operate under a strict code of "what is said here, stays here!" Help and support is offered for people who are trying to cope with living with a person who compulsively uses alcohol or with someone who is in recovery for alcohol abuse.

React and Respond

1. What do you think an addiction is? From your point of view, what is the difference between an addiction to a process and an addiction to a substance?

2. Why are addictions so difficult to overcome?

3. In Romans 7:18–20, the apostle Paul says, "I know that nothing good lives in me, that is, in my sinful nature. For I have the desire to do what is good, but I cannot carry it out. For what I do is not the good I want to do; no, the evil I do not want to do—this I keep on doing. Now if I do what I do not want to do, it is no longer I who do it, but it is sin living in me that does it." Have you ever experienced this kind of struggle in your life? How do you think this compares with the struggle of an alcoholic?

4. Form a small group of three or four. Without mentioning names, talk about the struggles of alcoholics or others you may know who have addictions. How do you think you can be most helpful to them?

5. "Who shall separate us from the love of Christ? Shall trouble or hardship or persecution or famine or nakedness or danger or sword? As it is written: 'For your sake we face death all day long; we are considered as sheep to be slaughtered.' No, in all these things we are more than conquerors through Him who loved us. For I am convinced that neither death nor life, neither angels nor demons, neither the present nor the future, nor any powers, neither height nor depth, nor anything else in all creation, will be able to separate us from the love of God that is in Christ Jesus our Lord" (Romans 8:35–39). Do you believe it would be possible for an addiction to separate a person from Christ and His unconditional love? Why or why not?

The Addictive Process

Susan and Kirk seemed like the perfect couple. They seemed to have everything—education, good and stable jobs, lovely children, a nice home on the edge of town, and they were accepted in and productive members of their community. Both of them had been social drinkers in college. Kirk admitted to being drunk often on weekends during college, but Susan had never really got drunk. Even though she admitted to drinking more than her share often enough, she always felt she was able to drive home.

Now, years after college, Kirk's drinking had become more frequent and intense. He was getting drunk most weekends, but only occasionally was he too hung over to go in to work on Monday mornings. Susan began to worry about their marriage because usually when they went anywhere socially, Kirk drank too much, Susan drove home, and they ended the evening in a fight.

Kirk began stopping off after work for a drink with the guys. He always argued that he was all right to drive, but Susan wondered. She was scared and said that they seldom argued about anything other than Kirk's drinking. After he received his first ticket for driving under the influence of an intoxicating substance, Susan got more scared and quit drinking completely.

Kirk began to stay away from home more and more and Susan found herself crying more and more. She felt lonely and depressed most of the time. He threatened to leave her if she didn't stop nagging about his drinking. And she threatened to leave him if he didn't stop drinking and scaring her so. Finally, he received his second alcohol-related driving offense when he was involved in a traffic accident. In addition to a stiff fine, Kirk was required by the court to attend classes intended to educate him about his relationship to alcohol and his responsibilities while driving.

The day of the first session Kirk was too sick to attend, and Susan refused to call and make another excuse for him. She simply walked away and left him lying in bed crying. She sought help from a friend who took her to a counselor and suggested they attend Al-anon together. Susan knew she too had become sick and needed to get better, even if Kirk didn't want to.

Alcoholism often begins with harmless social drinking. But because alcohol is a mood-altering chemical, continued and increased use of alcohol often alters a person's mood to the point that close and intimate relationships are damaged, often disrupted. Someone has said that it is difficult to be in love with someone who is in love with alcohol.

The first step is "We admitted that we were powerless over alcohol—that our lives had become unmanageable." John Dryden once said, "Ill habits gather by unseen degrees—as brooks make rivers, rivers run to seas!" Recovery from alcoholism begins when a person acknowledges powerlessness. The only person who can help an alcoholic is the alcoholic!

Alcoholism is a crippling disease. How would you tell if a person is an alcoholic? According to the principles of Alcoholics Anonymous, only that person can say for sure. But some signs of approaching danger are: trouble with family and other relationships and difficulties at work due to chemical or alcohol use. As the disease advances, alcoholics have "black outs," which include forgetting where they parked their car, where they were or who they were with the night before, or how they got home. While some people are "happy drunks" because alcohol is a mood altering chemical, others under alcohol's influence become argumentative and crabby.

At this point in the development of the disease, many alcoholics began to notice a terrible loneliness and an alienation from other people, but especially from those who question their drinking or their ability to handle alcohol. Finally it causes problems with their ability to do most other things, and the compulsion of drinking and getting the next drink becomes the most important thing in an individual's life.

There are many published checklists which can be used to help others determine whether or not a friend or relative has a problem with alcohol. But in the end, only that individual can make that decision. And that realization begins with an admission: "We admitted we were powerless over alcohol— that our lives had become unmanageable."

The steps are written in the first person plural because Bill W. and Dr. Bob believed that an alcoholic can only be helped by another alcoholic. And the development of the disease, while progressive, can be arrested when an individual truly wants and seeks help from another recovering addict. "We admitted we were powerless." Recovery begins when an addict hits bottom and realizes there is no where else to go.

React and Respond

1. Do you believe Kirk is an alcoholic? What would you do if you were Susan?

2. Alcohol is a mood-altering chemical. How does this help you understand some of the problems which occur in the life of an alcoholic?

3. It has been said that alcohol is only 10 percent of the problem in an alcoholic's life. What do you think the other 90 percent is?

Addiction to a Process

While much has been written about addiction to mood-altering substances such as alcohol and drugs, very little has been written about addiction to processes such as work, sex, and gambling. In one sense they are very similar. The same type of questions may be asked as those used to determine whether a person has a problem with alcohol. Do your excessive work habits cause problems in your personal life or professional life? Do you feel at times you lose control of your life? Do you feel lonely because of your work?

Many 12-step self-help groups have been begun which are patterned after Alcoholics Anonymous. Just as Bill W. and Dr. Bob dreamed, these groups offer individual addicts the possibility of receiving help from another recovering addict and, once on the road to recovery, of offering help and support to others. One such group, Workaholics Anonymous, was formed on the east coast in the early eighties. This group is made up of individuals who have a desire to stop acting out by compulsive working. Just as in addiction to alcohol, work addicts turn to a so-called Higher Power for help. The 12 steps are identical to those of AA, except that the word *work* is substituted in the first step, and few other changes denoting the difference in addiction in later steps.

The group offers the following "test" to determine the seriousness of a person's addiction to work. From your own perspective, answer yes or no to the following 20 questions. You could also do this for someone you love or are concerned about.

1. Do you get more excited about your work than about family or anything else?

2. Are there times when you can charge through your work and other times when you can't?

3. Do you take work with you to bed? on weekends? on vacation?

4. Is work the activity you like to do best and talk about the most?

5. Do you work more than 40 hours a week?

6. Do you turn your hobbies into money-making ventures?

7. Do you take complete responsibility for the outcome of your work efforts?

8. Have your family or friends given up expecting you on time?

9. Do you take on extra work because you are concerned that it won't otherwise get done?

10. Do you underestimate how long a project will take and then rush to complete it?

11. Do you believe that it is okay to work long hours if you love what you are doing?

12. Do you get impatient with people who have priorities other than work?

13. Are you afraid that if you don't work hard you will lose your job or be a failure?

14. Is the future a constant worry for you even when things are going very well?

15. Do you do things energetically and competitively, including play?

16. Do you get irritated when people ask you to stop doing your work in order to do something else?

17. Have your long hours hurt your family or other relationships?

18. Do you think about your work while driving, falling asleep, or when others are talking?

19. Do you work or read during meals?

20. Do you believe that more money will solve the other problems in your life?

(From "Workaholics Anonymous: A Brief Guide." Used by permission.)

If you answered yes to more than a three or more of the questions, you may have a problem with work. If you answered yes to more than half of the questions, there is a good chance that you do have a problem with work. And what if the problem is with someone else? What can you do? As is the case with alcoholism, only the alcoholic can effect a change in individual behavior. If you are concerned about your own behavior, you may consider one of the following courses of action.

- Read a book about compulsive working such as *Work Addiction* by Bryan E. Robinson, (Deerfield Beach, Florida: Health Communications, Inc., 1989), or *Working Ourselves To Death,* by Diane Fassel, (New York: Harper Collins, 1990).

- Find a 12-step group such as WA to help you. Because Workaholics Anonymous groups are not nearly as numerous or widespread as AA groups, you may have trouble locating a group in your area. If you are interested, you can contact the World Service Organization for WA at P.O. Box 289, Menlo Park, CA 94026-0289 or leave a message at 510-273-9253. If you cannot locate a group near you, you could consider starting a group. The World Service Organization also provides organizational materials to help you get started. You could attend an AA meeting and ask for help in getting started.

What if you have read these test questions with a friend or loved one in mind? What if your concern is for someone else? What then? First of all, be aware that you can't make someone else recover from any addiction. Only God can do that. Secondly, realize that just as an individual is powerless over the substance or process of his/her addiction. You are also powerless to change that person. Perhaps the best you can hope for is that by effecting a change in yourself, the other person may change. You may need to move on from an ever-sickening relationship with an addict who refuses to change.

Read some of the myths which Diane Fassel lists in her book and see if you can determine why they are myths.

1. Only employed people are workaholics.
2. Workaholism only affects high-powered executives and yuppies.
3. Workaholism is only stress and burnout.

4. Workaholism can be "managed" with stress-reduction techniques.
5. No one ever died of hard work.
6. Workaholism is profitable for corporations.
7. Workaholism is a positive addiction.
8. Workaholics are superproductive—they get ahead.
9. Workaholism only adversely affects the workaholic.
10. Workaholics are happy.

("10 Myths and Reasons [paraphrased] Why They Are Myths" from *Working Ourselves to Death* by Diane Fassel. Copyright © 1990 by Diane Fassel. Reprinted by permission of HarperCollins Publishers, Inc.)

How did you do? Do you know why these are myths? Here are some reasons.

1. Even unemployed and retired people can overwork. It depends on one's attitude toward work and activity.
2. People from every social and economic class do suffer work addiction.
3. Compared to other addictions, workaholism is clearly a process of being out of control in relationship to a process that is cumulative and progressive. Where an alcoholic can quit drinking all alcoholic beverages, a workaholic probably can't stop working entirely. It's like trying to recover while still drinking!
4. Workaholism does fit the definition of an addiction, and those who fit the patterns of the 12-steps, the questions, and the myths will probably need to take steps to move away from the overfunctioning behavior. They probably can't stop working!
5. No one ever died of hard work, but stress related diseases are epidemic in nature in our country. In Japan, there is even a special word in the vocabulary describing someone who "works themselves to death."
6. In the end, companies actually lose when they applaud the overworking of the their employees. The costs of retraining to replace those who quit, die, or get smart and move into a different job are tremendous.
7. Many people who agree that substance abuse is negative may tend to see work addiction as positive. But there is no such thing as a positive process which becomes increasingly controlling and ultimately destructive. No addiction, by definition, can be considered positive.

8. Workaholics may appear to be superproductive, but in the end, they actually produce less than the person who just plods along. Compare the truths of the story of the tortoise and the hare.
9. No one is an island. We always affect others—usually those closest to us.
10. True workaholics may appear to be happy and tell you they are happy doing what they do. But examine the balance in their lives. Consider how seldom a workaholic actually plays as a sign of the development of their disease.

Many people will applaud the pain which a work addict goes through in order to earn the title of "superproductive." But if they truly understood the danger and frustration of working out of control, they would pray for these individuals instead of encouraging them. That is why the Serenity Prayer is so important. "God grant me serenity!"

John found that his commute to and from work was eating up too much of his precious time. So, reluctantly, he told his wife and kids that in order to devote more time to his business he was actually moving out of the house and into his office. And he did. During this period of separation, his wife hung on, despite his encouragement from friends to divorce him. She desperately hoped that he would realize the danger of his lifestyle and begin to recover.

It is hard to believe an addiction can become so pervasive and dangerous. People who study addictions admit that an addiction is illogical behavior which has gone amuck. Work addicts must confront their overfunctioning for the disease and/or addiction that it is.

Because of His love in Christ, God has given us gifts and asks us to use them to His glory. As we enjoy the God-given gift of time, God would have us thank Him for it and value it as one of our most precious resources.

React and Respond

1. What does it mean that "work addiction is the only lifeboat that is guaranteed to sink"?

2. With another person, discuss any of the test questions which you answered in the affirmative and about which you have some concern.

3. Apply the following to addictive behaviors: "Of them the proverbs are true, 'A dog returns to its vomit,' and, 'A sow that is washed goes back to her wallowing in the mud' " (2 Peter 2:22). Discuss how, according to the following, Christ has redeemed and set you free. "For He has rescued us from the dominion of darkness and brought us into the kingdom of the Son He loves, in whom we have redemption, the forgiveness of sins" (Colossians 1:13–14).

6 Fostering Friendships

To Have a Friend You Have to Be a Friend

(Ring, ring, ring) "Hi, this is Tony. Can't get to the phone just now, but I'd like to hear what you have to say. So, you know the program—leave a message, and I'll get back to you sometime soon" *(beep)*.

"Hey, Tony. This is Manuel. How about joining us for golf at Hillcrest, tonight at 6:00? Sig is out of town, and our regular sub is sick. How about it? Let me know. I'll be in the office till 3:00, in the car till 5:00, or you can page me. You know the numbers. Bye" *(beep)*.

(Ring, ring, ring) "Hi, this is Manuel, and I don't know who you are—so if you'd please identify yourself as well as let me in on what you want, I'll get with you just as soon as I can. So long!"*(beep)*.

"So, Manuel—its before 3:00, and you're not in. But I am, and I'm good to go for golf at 6:00. But where is Hillcrest? Didn't we play at Southview last time? Call me—I'll be in the office until 5:00, and then I'll have to rush to join you on the tee. Lucky guy. Must be nice to work only part of the day" *(beep)*!

(Ring, ring, ring) "Hi, this is Tony ... ."

"Hey, Tony. Long time no hear. Is this really you? Or, am I still talking to your machine?"

"No, it's me—live and in person. So, you don't remember where Hillcrest is? You've been out of circulation in this part of town for too long."

"Ya, ya, ya. Just give me the scoop and let me get back to work. I've got a lot to finish before I can leave work."

"Oh, okay. Sorry. It's out south on McKnight, off 36. It will be good to see you again. It's been a month or more, hasn't it?"

"Just about. Hey, thanks for inviting me. See you in a bit. Fly low and until then, buddy. Bye."

"Bye" *(click)*.

The marvels of modern technology certainly make friendships something other than they used to be. We can keep track of one another at home, at work, while driving in our car, or flying across the country. Some pager systems boast worldwide coverage. It's like we never need to be out of touch with those who are important to us. All the more reason to make frequent real, human connection.

Friendship and human contact are very important. Newborn children develop and mature positively if they are touched, caressed, and talked to. Those who are ignored or even reinforced negatively tend to be withdrawn and leery or hostile toward human contact. We all have a basic human need to be loved and cared for by others.

What does it take to have friends? Some people have many, while others seem to have only a few. Some people seem to come into their own at large social gatherings; others derive greater enjoyment from casual conversation with one or two others.

Some people immerse themselves in a flurry of parties and social obligations. They are so busy that they may not have time to form close, lasting relationships. Others have never ventured to risk losing a friend, and remain alone. One person remarked that he had experienced so much pain in saying good-bye to friends that he finally stopped saying hello! But Tennyson offered another perspective. At the death of his friend A. H. Hallam, he declared, " 'Tis better to have loved and lost than never to have loved at all!"

In reality, no one can have really close relationships with more than a few people. Relationships take time. And in the end, you have to be a friend to have friends. People who sit around, feeling lonely and sorry for themselves, may have never tasted the joys of a close friendship because they have been unwilling to expend the time and energy required to make and keep friends.

Our loving God designed us to live in relationship with one another and with Him. Jesus said it this way, "Greater love has no one than this—that he lay down his life for his friends" (John 15:13). But don't just listen to Jesus' words. Watch Him. He was almost always around people. He sought them out. He offered Himself to them. And finally He gave Himself totally, for you and me—as the ultimate friend, He gave His life on our behalf. "I am the good shepherd. I know My sheep and My sheep know Me—just as the Father knows Me and I know the Father—and I lay down My life for the sheep" (John 10:14–15).

Some people struggle in establishing and building relationships because of the "unfinished business" from their families of origin. Examine your family of origin and ask whether your family members were close to or distant from one another. Examine your role in the social structure of the family. This may begin to help unlock the key to your relationships. It may also help you understand yourself and your relationships with others.

A story is told about twin sisters. One was very popular and outgoing. The other was quiet and stayed at home most of the time. After they matured, they each shared that they envied the other. Each wished she were more or less popular. The outgoing sister later confided that her social position in school put a lot of expectations and pressures upon her, many of which she felt she could not live up to. She said she admired her sister for her quiet control. The shy retiring sister admired her sister's outgoing nature, but said she always felt insecure.

Each of us can find confidence and encouragement knowing that because of what Jesus has done for us on Calvary, we have God's approval. "If anyone is in Christ, he is a new creation." (2 Corinthians 5:17). In the shed blood of Christ, God has remade us. Despite our flaws, and the failures of the past, God has given us a new lease on life. And then He has sent us out into the world to win others. One Bible translation puts it this way: "Since God is pleading through us, we are ambassadors for Christ. We ask you for Christ. 'Come and be God's friends'" (2 Corinthians 5:20 An American Translation). How do you appeal to others to be God's friends? How do you appeal with others to be your friend?

React and Respond

1. Is it easier or more difficult to establish and maintain friendships in today's world than in former times?

2. What evidence do you have that in spite of the distance people often place between themselves and others, they still crave close human contact?

3. Find a partner and share the role your friends play in your life. If you were to change something about your friends and their role in your life, what would it be?

4. In examining your family of origin, what have you learned about the way you relate to others?

5. Why did Jesus lay down His life for you? How do you give of yourself for others?

David and Jonathan

A long time ago there were two young men, Jonathan and David. Jonathan was a wealthy prince; his father, Saul, was king. David lived a much simpler life. His father, Jesse, owned livestock and David worked as a shepherd. Jonathan was to all human appearances, successor to the throne, but God had other plans. He sent the prophet Samuel to anoint David as the next king. These two young men might well have been enemies, yet they fast became friends. "Jonathan made a covenant with David because he loved him as himself. Jonathan took off the robe he was wearing and gave it to David, along with his tunic, and even his sword, his bow and his belt" (1 Samuel 18:3–4).

King Saul was jealous of David's victories in the battlefield and wanted to kill David. But Jonathan warned David to flee and defended David to his father, begging him not to try to kill David. Finally, when he realized that his father would not listen to him, Jonathan vowed to defend his friend with his life. (See 1 Samuel 19:6.)

David was forced to flee. Their final farewell on a hill outside of Jerusalem is a very touching tribute to strong friendship. (See 1 Samuel 20:42.) What can you learn about friendship from the relationship between David and Jonathan? It was almost like a strange force drew them together and deepened their friendship. But it's not really such a mystery. The binding force in their relationship was a deep faith in the Lord.

Jonathan loved David just like he loved himself. God's summary of the Two Tables of the Law speaks of this same kind of love. "Love the Lord your God with all your heart and with all your soul and with all your strength and with all your mind, and, 'Love your neighbor as yourself' " (Luke 10:27). This kind of loyalty and love grows out of the unity they shared because of their common faith.

Although they had grown up differently, Jonathan accepted David as an equal. Friends become equals even when circumstances make it difficult. Jonathan and David were friends in the best sense of the word. They could unashamedly say they loved each other. And they showed it.

React and Respond

1. What are your impressions about the friendship between David and Jonathan? What have you learned about friendship from them?

2. Tell about a good friend in your life.

3. Consider Jonathan's covenant with David and his promise, "Whatever you want me to do, I'll do for you" (1 Samuel 20:4). How many relationships do you have like that? Talk about the value of building friendships with other Christians.

Who Are Your Friends?

In his book *The Friendship Factor,* (Minneapolis: Augsburg, 1979), Dr. Alan Loy McGinnis suggests placing a priority on relationships. He encourages taking time for those who are really important to you—especially within your family. You can determine the number and quality of friendships by asking the following questions:
1. Do you have at least one person nearby whom you can call on in times of personal distress?
2. Do you have several people whom you can visit with little advance warning without apology?
3. Do you have several people with whom you can share recreational activities?
4. Do you have people who will lend you money if you need it, or those who will care for you in practical ways if the need arises?
5. Do you have one person whom you would feel comfortable calling if you had a problem at three o'clock in the morning?

(Reprinted from *The Friendship Factor* by Alan Loy McGinnis, copyright © 1979 Augsburg Publishing House. Used by permission of Augsburg Fortress.)

Friends are a tremendous gift from God, cherished because of the encouragement, support, and joy they bring to our lives. Yet, because we are sinners, at times we take our friends for granted. We may even come to regard relationships and ultimately other people as useful for a time and then disposable. God has given us things to use and people to love. But we can easily get these priorities reversed, using people and loving objects.

God in Christ has forgiven our abuse of the relationships He has given us. By the power of His Spirit He enables us to take the risk necessary to reach out to others in sacrificial acts of friendship, the same kind of friendship His Son went to the ultimate extreme to establish with us.

React and Respond

1. Harold S. Kushner has said, "Our society has trained men to be comfortable with competition and uncomfortable with intimacy." Do you agree or disagree? Why?

2. How do you show relationships with others to be a priority in your life?

3. Do you ever use people and love things? How does the power and strength of God's Spirit bring us to relate to others?

Friends in Deed

You can count on true friends in good times and in bad. There are several other important signs of friendship. Friends let you know them—they are somehow available to you. They ask about you, and they tell you about themselves. The most important thing you can do for someone is to ask about their life. The next most important thing is to listen to what they have to say. Let them know you care. Jesus talked about love and then went to the cross to demonstrate it. One of Jesus' friends and close followers said it this way. "Dear children, let us not love with words or tongue but with actions and in truth." (1 John 3:18). In other words, "Let's put our whole selves into it."

There is a big difference between the words love and like. You may like candy or a new car. But you can't truly love candy or a car. Love requires a personal relationship. Just as we get turned around and use people and love objects, we get love and like turned around. We can turn our affections toward things or events such as work, recreational, and work activities and shut out people and relationships.

God gives us friends so we can build them up and they can build us up. Jesus encourages another aspect of true friendships—honesty, mutual accountability, and loving confrontation. Jesus says, "If your brother sins against you, go and show him his fault" (Matthew 18:15). He doesn't say, "If your brother does something you don't like, then it's okay to tell several others." Jesus urged personal, one-on-one interaction, always motivated by love with a goal that the friendship will be retained, and the friend may once again become close to you.

In a case like this, why do you think it is important to confront an individual one-on-one? Why not tell others and make the person feel guilty enough to repent? This is manipulation not love. Mature relationships are based on honesty and openness. In a healthy relationship we admit that we cannot change another person. We can only report to them how we feel about what they have done or said.

When in your relationships do you need to speak the truth in love? Although often ignored or discounted, the Bible contains many helpful suggestions for maintaining mature and healthy relationships. "Therefore each one of you must put off falsehood and speak truthfully to his neighbor, for we are all members of one body. In your anger, do not sin. Do not let the sun go down while you are still angry, and do not give the devil a foothold." (Ephesians 4:25–27)

In words which explain the Eighth Commandment, "You shall not give false testimony against your neighbor," we are encouraged to "explain everything in the kindest way." This is very hard, but it is the most constructive way to build and maintain healthy relationships.

React and Respond

1. In cultivating friendships, when is it important for you to "tell it like it is"?

2. What are the differences between the words love and like? Do you find it hard to love someone you don't like? What about Jesus? How did He love the unlovable?

3. Why is it important to confront someone privately about their sin? What harm could come if your private confrontation became public knowledge?

4. Some conversations consist not in listening to the other person and responding but in thinking up stories to top what the other person is talking about. What does the following statement say about true friendship? "The true spirit of conversation consists in building on another man's observations, not overturning it" (Edward G. Bulwer-Lytton).

5. What happens if you don't share your feelings both positive and negative with others? How do you feel about the following statement "Holding on to anger is like grasping a hot coal with the intent of throwing it at someone else—yet you are the one who gets burned."

Good Friends

Gale Sayers and Brian Piccolo were both running backs on the Chicago Bears football team. In 1967, when they began rooming together, this was an important first for both men. Sayers was black and had never had a close relationship with a white person. And Piccolo had never known a black person by name.

While rooming together, they became close and lasting friends. They both also had a tremendous sense of humor and were not above playing tricks on each another. But beneath the surface of the humor lay a fierce loyalty. Two years later Piccolo was stricken with cancer and spent most of the season sick and in hospitals. Whenever possible, his huge black friend flew to Piccolo's side and comforted him. All season they had planned to sit together, with their wives, at the Professional Football Writers annual dinner where they were both to be given an award for the most courageous player in professional football. But Brian Piccolo, confined to a hospital bed, could not be there.

When Sayers, who ordinarily did not show his emotions publicly, stood to receive his award, his eyes suddenly filled with tears. He said, unashamedly, "You flatter me by giving me this award. But I tell you here and now that I accept it for Brian Piccolo. Brian Piccolo is the man of courage who should receive the George S. Hallas Award. I love Brian Piccolo, and I'd like you to love him. Tonight, when you hit your knees, please ask God to love him too!" (from *The Friendship Factor*, page 41).

To how many people can you say, "I love you"? And when

do you say it openly and publicly? Do you wait until they are on their death bed? Do you let those who are your friends know that you love them? With God's power we can learn to tell them openly and straight up. And we can cultivate a lifestyle that makes it easy to show them too.

React and Respond

1. Why was the relationship between Sayers and Piccolo so unlikely in 1967? What brings people together? What keeps them apart?

2. How important are close relationships to you? Evaluate this saying: "We tend to define ourselves by our earning power not by our human connections." As you think about people you know, who possesses a wealth of friends?

3. Is there someone to whom you would like say "I love you!"? Pray and ask God to give you the courage to be open to your family and friends about your love for them. What can you do to thank God for your friendships?

ANSWERS AND COMMENTS

It Is Good!

At the Lake

React and Respond

1. Answers will vary. Affirm all responses.

2. Again, accept all responses. For some, the time for talking with God may be early in the morning or late at night when everything is quiet.

The Gift of Leisure

React and Respond

1. Answers will vary. Encourage participants to explain their answers.

2. Answers will vary. Most likely, participants will comment that their lives are more complicated and harried than those of their parents and grandparents.

Time, the Commodity

React and Respond

1. Encourage participants to share about the ideas about rest and relaxation they learned from their parents and other significant adults in their lives. Affirm all responses.

2. Answers will vary.

3. Comment that the difference between a "human being" and a "human doing" is that the words *human being* emphasize an individual's personhood. The term *human doing* seems to define a person according to what he or she does.

4. Affirm responses. Point out that God is the one who is in control of all things, despite our preoccupation with the completion of tasks and the meeting of obligations and commitments. We can rest assured, knowing that ultimately He is in control of all things.

In God We Rest

React and Respond

1. In worship we receive God's blessings through the Word in the Scripture readings, sermon, assurance of our forgiveness, and as we gather around the Lord's Table and the baptismal font. In worship we also respond to God's goodness to us in Christ Jesus in our songs, hymns, and prayers.

We worship God individually and as part of a faith community. Stress the importance of worshiping God together with our brothers and sisters in Christ.

2. Emphasize the importance of assembling for corporate worship. Although we worship God when we pray to Him and otherwise celebrate the marvels of His created world, we miss the blessings of fellowship, service, nurture, and others when we neglect public worship.

3. Accept responses. The Sabbath is a time set aside by God and dedicated by Him for our physical and spiritual rest and refreshment. Jesus is our Sabbath rest. He provided our rescue from the slavery of sin, death, and the devil's power. Ultimately, we will enjoy the perfect refreshment of heaven where our energy will never abate.

4. Accept responses. Comment that we can worship God at all times and in a variety of ways. By the Spirit's power the entire life of a Christian is and can be an expression of worship.

Temple Maintenance

Ivor and Jane and Harry and Sally

1. Encourage participant responses. Invite the group to share about how God is working in our lives during lean and troubled times to remind us of His love and presence and care.

2. Again, encourage participant responses. Most likely participants will find it easy to relate to the hurried, hectic, and fast-paced lives of Harry and Sally.

3. Accept responses.

Exercise

React and Respond

1. Accept participant responses. Affirm that people respond and react to work in various ways. For many it gives life meaning; for others, work provides the means to purchasing power for the needs and wants of life.

2. Answers will vary. Point out that stress can be both positive and negative. Stress can provide the motivating force behind excellence as well as the cause of headaches, frustration, and despair.

3. Answers will vary.

4. Accept participants' responses. Point out that bringing our bodies under the control of the Holy Spirit honors God as it demonstrates the growing faith in our lives. Comment that the Spirit brings love, joy, peace, patience, kindness, goodness, faithfulness, gentleness, and self-control into our lives as He works through Word and Sacrament.

5. Stress that Jesus paid the ultimate price for us and our salvation: He died, taking upon Himself the punishment we deserved because of our sins. We respond to His goodness to us as we honor Him with the proper care and maintenance of our bodies, which are His temple since by faith the Holy Spirit dwells within them.

Let's Get Moving

React and Respond

1. Accept participant responses.

2. Answers will vary.

3. Emphasize the goodness of God; He continually works things for the good of His people. Even sweat, which Genesis 3:19 associates with the fall into sin, is good for the human body receives healthful conditioning through exercise.

Bodily Care in Perspective

React and Respond

1. Exercise and preoccupation with the care and appearance of our bodies could become a form of idolatry if carried to an extreme.

2. Answers will vary. If exercise receives more time and attention in the life of a believer than God, exercise has become too high of a priority.

3. Accept participant responses. Many affirm the value of exercise and recreational activities that can be enjoyed throughout life, such as bowling, golf, and hunting.

Running to Win

React and Respond

1. The Holy Spirit is the third person of the Trinity. Much of what we know about the Holy Spirit centers around His work. 1 Corinthians 6:11 reminds us, "You were washed, you were sanctified, you were justified in the name of the Lord Jesus Christ and by the Spirit of our God." The Holy Spirit brings us faith and builds and sustains the saving faith within us as He works through Word and Sacrament in our lives.

2. Comment that only by the Spirit's power are we motivated and enabled to "run to win" in the life we live for Jesus. Answers will vary.

3. Answers will vary. Affirm that God make us each as unique creations, individually formed and designed by our wonderful creator. Just as He has gifted us in a variety of ways, He equips us for a variety of ways in which to serve Him.

4. Answers will vary. Comment that our God is the God of new beginnings. In the forgiveness and strength He daily provides, He enables us continually to begin anew in our thoughts, in our actions, and in our identity as His sons.

Living a Balanced Life

A Look at a Life

React and Respond

1. The author reflects that if he had his life to live over again, he would enjoy it more, rounding out his cautious personality by being more spontaneous and fun-loving. Agreement with the author's perspective may depend, at least in part, on whether individuals match the author's personality type.

2. Answers will vary.

Rest and Rust!

React and Respond

1. Accept participant responses as to what they do for a change of pace as a diversion from work.

2. Answers will vary.

3. Again, answers will vary according to individual personalities and preferences.

4. Machines may excel at performing automatic routine functions. People offer creativity, humor, dedication, care, and concern in their approach to tasks.

5. God made us for community. He desires us to build relationships with one another. He empowers us to share His Word—Law and Gospel—in the relationships we build.

Rest Is Repair

React and Respond

1. Encourage participants to share about times when they have worked to excess and how they felt as a result.

2. Our bodies require rest and nourishment in order to be productive. Machines have only certain designated functions to perform. They run as long as they have an energy source.

3. Allow time for participants to respond. Invite them to share their conclusions with the others in the group.

Our Daily Bread

React and Respond

1. Accept participant responses about work and rest and their plan for and participation in leisure activities.

2. God blessed the seventh day so that we could receive rest and renewal for both our bodies and our souls.

3. Answers will vary. Participants will affirm the negative consequences of not maintaining a proper balance between rest and work.

4. Affirm participant responses.

5. God wants to underscore for His people of all time that we are dependent on Him for all we need, want, and otherwise receive in our lives.

Life Patterns

React and Respond

1. Answers will vary. Comment that just as we learn from others without their consciously intending to teach us, we are continually teaching others, though we may be unaware of whom we are teaching and how we are teaching.

2. Accept participant comments. Encourage them to think about how they fulfill this role as husbands, fathers, coaches, scout leaders, etc.

Lighten Up!

React and Respond

1. Answers will vary. Fatigue, irritability, lack of attention to detail, susceptibility to illness and other indicators may signal a work overload.

2. Affirm the power, strength, and encouragement Jesus brings to our lives and His invitation to help us carry our burdens (Matthew 11:28–29).

3. We witness to others about the faith and hope that is ours in Jesus when we talk to them about how He gives us strength and encouragement as we face the future.

4. The forgiveness Jesus earned for us on Calvary's tree is the basis for our relationship with God and the relationships we establish and build with those around us.

Healthy Hobbies

"Get a Life!"

React and Respond

1. Good counselors don't generally advise. Rather, they walk with individuals through the issues that trouble and concern them, helping them to see how they might decide to progress beyond their immediate problem or confronting issue to find a new and revised direction in their lives. Most likely the counselor will help Sam to recognize his need to find fulfillment and meaning in his life in a way different from that which he had originally planned. Most friends would help Sam by inviting him to become involved in activi-

ties and interests he is likely to enjoy. Christian friends could invite him to increase his involvement in the life of the congregation.

2. Hobbies provide a change of pace from the issues and challenges of the work-a-day world. This change of pace can carry over into retirement in a significant way because hobbies remain to enrich a person's life even after he has retired.

3. Healthy hobbies are those which help to bring fulfillment, satisfaction, and the enjoyment to our lives in ways that help us to appreciate the world God has made. They also make a positive contribution to our own lives and the lives of those around us. Unhealthy hobbies are those things that consume time and interests yet weaken our health, our relationships, or our positive sense of self as men of God.

Who Are You?

React and Respond

1. Encourage volunteers to share the things they hope define them to others.

2. We get to know ourselves better by planning activities that help us to build relationships with others or simply to reflect on ourselves and our life's goals, direction, and accomplishments. God strengthens and directs us as we read and study His Word and talk to Him in prayer. Setting aside a time for study, prayer, and reflection—either privately or in the company of family and friends—we invite God's continued guidance and encouragement in our lives.

3. Accept student responses. Encourage participants to explore various ways they may expand and enrich their lives through the development of new hobbies and interests.

The Origin of Interests

React and Respond

1. Encourage participants to share about the positive role models in their lives. Comment that most people come to enjoy hobbies that are also of interest to those close to them.

2. Reinforce the idea that we learn much about our approach to work and leisure from our family of origin. Accept and affirm all responses.

3. Again encourage participants to share. Answers will vary.

Hobbies and Pastimes in Modern Times

React and Respond

1. Many will note that they have—and notice in others—differences in personality, approach, and expectations between when they are at work and when they are at home or engaged in leisure activities.

2. God is with us at all times. He invites us always to trust in His power and presence and to communicate with Him regularly in all we do. Answers to the question will vary. Point out that God's love and care are constants. If we relate to God differently at work than when at leisure or at various stages of life, it is because we are looking at things from a different perspective rather than the presence of any change in God.

3. Point out that play energizes and invigorates us when we participate in it, stimulating our creativity and refreshing us for the new and routine tasks awaiting us.

Let's Go Fishing

React and Respond

1. Perhaps Jesus was setting the stage for the miracle He was about to perform to remind them to depend on Him.

2. Encourage participant sharing. Many will probably relate to feeling guilty when they are relaxing. Brainstorm ways to move beyond feelings of guilt over taking time to relax by ourselves or in the company of family and friends. Remind participants that God created rest on the seventh day.

3. Invite the group to share following the directions included in this item. "Prime the pump" by sharing what Jesus' power and presence means in your life.

4. Invite the group to share. This question invites comments about how well we deal with changes in plans and the prospect of spending an unplanned quiet evening at home.

5. Invite participant sharing. Ask the group to define a "time-robber." Accept diverse opinions as to what activities are "time-robbers."

6. Accept responses.

Addictive Behaviors: Misuses of Leisure Time

The Crazy Man Driving My Bus!

React and Respond

1. Answers will vary. All of us at times feel the pressures of life closing in around us.

2. Accept participant responses. As the chapter affirms, one of the advantages of classifying alcoholism as a disease is that with this designation many insurance companies will financially assist persons struggling with alcohol addiction to receive help.

3. God our Savior invites us to "Cast all [our] anxiety on Him because He cares for [us]" (1 Peter 5:7). God's forgiveness covers all sins, including those associated with addictions. He wiped the slate clean for us on Calvary's cross, even as we continue to face and live with the addiction itself and its consequences.

Addiction: Denial of Powerlessness

React and Respond

1. Anne Wilson Schaef and Diane Fassel of The Addictive Organization define addiction as "any substance or process that has taken over our lives and over which we are powerless." Addiction to a substance is to become dependent on a chemical, addiction to a process is to become dependent on an action.

2. Addictions are difficult to overcome because we have come to rely on them in order to function.

3. Paul's word describing sin and the control it holds over every human echoes in the life of every chemically dependent person who desires to be free of a substance's control. Allow participants to reflect on the struggle involved in alcoholism.

4. Encourage participants to share their knowledge, experience, and insights about addiction and its devastating consequences. We help those who struggle in this way by supporting them in their desire to be free of the substance controlling them and by encouraging them in their decision to receive help.

5. Christ's love is stronger than the power of any addiction. Nothing can ever separate us from Jesus and His love. Jesus' love remains—forgiving, restoring, and empowers all who by faith belong to Him including those who struggle with addiction.

The Addictive Process

React and Respond

1. It appears obvious from the description that alcohol has an unhealthy influence in Kirk's life. Most likely Kirk suffers from an addiction to alcohol. Susan may seek professional help to organize an intervention, an experience in which those closest to Kirk would confront him about his drinking and encourage him to seek to make healthy changes in his life.

2. Persons struggling with addiction to alcohol will often react to situations differently than they would if not under the influence. Alcohol addiction is often accompanied by domestic violence and other forms of abuse or neglect.

3. Tied to the abuse of alcohol in a person's life are the corresponding affects of manipulative behavior, neglect, and abuse on the chemically dependent person's life and relationships including his or her relationship with God.

Addiction to a Process

React and Respond

1. This expression means that although work is necessary to support and sustain life, work addicts can literally work themselves to death—sacrificing health, happiness, and relationships, and life itself.

2. Encourage participants to share about possible work addiction in their own life or in the lives of those close to them.

3. Addictive behaviors constantly draw the addicted person back under the power of the addiction. Underscore the freeing power of Christ Jesus—the "higher power" who has rescued us from the dominion of darkness through the forgiveness of sins. God's power enables us to "put on the new self, which is being renewed in knowledge in the image of its Creator" (Colossians 3:10).

Fostering Friendships

To Have a Friend You Have to Be a Friend

React and Respond

1. Accept responses, encouraging participants to explain their responses.

2. The human inclination to seek out relationships is evidenced by attendance at sporting events and conventions; the existence of clubs, churches, organizations, and associations; and our desire to connect ourselves through marriage and family relationships.

3. Accept participant responses.

4. Answers will vary. Encourage participant sharing about the influence their families have had on the relationships they establish.

5. Jesus gave His life unconditionally on our behalf to win our victory over sin, death, and the devil and to provide us with forgiveness of sins, new life, and eternal salvation. His power and love motivate us to give of ourselves unconditionally to all others, even strangers and enemies.

David and Jonathan

React and Respond

1. David and Jonathan were the best of friends. They demonstrated a Christlike affinity for one another. They did not hesitate to verbalize their affection for one another and to show their friendship in their sacrificial actions for one another.

2. Encourage participants to share about their friendships.

3. Encourage participants to share about the value of relationships in which all involved share and support one another in their love of Jesus. In such friendships believers support, encourage, forgive, and challenge one another in relationships rooted in the Gospel.

Who Are Your Friends?

React and Respond

1. Accept participants' responses. Most would concur that men and boys have been trained to compete, whereas girls are brought up to build and foster relationships.

2. Answers will likely include spending time talking with family and friends, planning and taking part in activities and events with those whose company we enjoy, taking time to listen to those who want to talk with us, seeking out others in order to build friendships with them.

3. Encourage participant responses. As God's Spirit works in our lives through the Word, He leads us to give of ourselves unconditionally for others.

Friends in Deed

React and Respond

1. As friendships grow, we are able to ask for, receive, and give honest feedback to friends without them becoming hurt or defensive. We can count on friends to have our best interests at heart.

2. The word *love* is used to express a devotion to someone with whom we have a relationship. The word *like* is best used to describe our favorable feelings about objects or activities. Jesus loved all people. His love found its basis not in our worth or attractiveness but rather in His holy, merciful, and benevolent nature.

3. God's Spirit moves us to treat others as we desire to be treated. Talking with others privately about a problem or concern keeps the focus on the issue and deals with it in the most direct and effective manner.

4. We show that we value the person to whom we are talking by honoring and affirming their opinions and experiences, rather than in our attempts to outdo them or diminish them.

5. Communication is vital and essential for maintaining healthy relationships. Encourage participants to explore the meaning and application of the quote on anger.

True Friends

React and Respond

1. Their relationship defied racial barriers. People are brought together by their common interests and needs and by the experiences they share. People are kept apart by prejudice, ignorance, and by isolating themselves from one another.

2. Participants may agree or disagree with the statement. Encourage them to share about someone they know who possesses a wealth of friends.

3. Underscore the importance of communicating our feelings within relationships. We thank God for our friends by demonstrating our appreciation for them in our prayers, by telling others that we value their friendship, and by our acting on our friendship in the lives we live for others in Jesus' name.